Jonas Hanway's
Scurrilous, Scandalous, Shockingly Sensational
Umbrella

Josh Crute

illustrated by Eileen Ryan Ewen

PAGE
STREET
KIDS

London was a rainy place,
no matter which way you said it.

On some days, it drizzled.
On others, it mizzled.
On others, it pelted and showered and spat.

When that happened, the only options were to
stay indoors, travel by coach, or just get wet.

By 1750, the people had gotten used to it.
"It's just what we do," they said.

Jonas Hanway did not agree.

He was a grumpy man
who disliked change as a general rule.

When something became popular that he didn't like,
he was never quiet about it.

But there was one thing that Jonas liked less than change.

And that was getting wet.

On rainy days,
he would pull on his thickest boots,
button up his sturdiest coat,
and throw on his largest hat.

Yet no matter how
fast he walked . . .

or which route he took,
when he arrived at his destination,

his socks were soggy,
his shirt was soaked,
and his wig looked like a wet cat.

"This simply won't do," he said.
So he left London . . .

and traveled the world

searching for a place where it never rained,

until he came to Persia.

And there, in the court of the shah,
he saw something strange.

It was SCURRILOUS! SCANDALOUS! SHOCKINGLY SENSATIONAL!

Or was it?

In reality, it wasn't so strange.
Umbrellas were ancient.
They could be found in cities all over the world.

But not in London.

The people of London thought
they were silly and foreign and frilly.
"It's not what we do," they said.

Jonas Hanway did not agree.

So, on one particular mizzling, drizzling, pelting, showering, spitting day, a scurrilous, scandalous, shockingly sensational thing happened.
Jonas Hanway stepped out of his house on Queen Square . . .

with an umbrella.

Ladies gasped. Gentlemen frowned.
Children giggled and said, "Mum, what is *that*?"

But when Jonas got to his destination, his socks were warm, his shirt was dry, and his wig looked like a fluffy cloud.

"This will do!" he said.

Jonas began to carry his umbrella everywhere.

Whenever he passed, people would laugh and say,

**"There goes that mad
Jonas Hanway."**

But the coach drivers were not laughing.
"This simply won't do," they said.
If everyone carried umbrellas,
then who would need their coaches when it rained?

So they jeered Jonas.

They threw rubbish at him.

One even tried to run him over.

But they could not stop Jonas.
He carried that umbrella
for *thirty years*, until one day . . .

a scurrilous, scandalous,
shockingly sensational thing
happened that surprised even Jonas.

Another umbrella popped up on the street.

And then another.

And another.

Soon, umbrellas were everywhere, dotting the city
from Greenwich Park to Hampstead Heath.

Today, London is still a rainy place,
no matter which way you say it.

On some days, it tipples.
On others, it dripples.
On others, it plothers and lutters and chucks.

But thanks to Jonas Hanway and his sensational umbrella, the people of London stay dry.

"It's just what we do," they say.

SCANDALOUS!

It may seem silly to us, but in 1750 it was considered unthinkable for an English gentleman like Jonas Hanway to carry an umbrella. Why? The answer lies in the phrase, "English gentleman." Jonas was a man, and umbrellas were thought to be for women. Jonas was also a *gentleman*, which meant he had money. Umbrellas were thought to be for people who were too poor to afford a coach or coach fare. And, most important, Jonas was English, and umbrellas were popular in France, a country that the English did not get along with.

HEADSTRONG HANWAY

When Jonas Hanway saw something he didn't like, he was never quiet about it! Here are two more times he fought to either resist change or effect it.

Umbrellas may not have been popular in England, but drinking tea sure was! Tea-rooms were popping up all over London, and "afternoon tea" was quickly becoming the new English tradition. Jonas Hanway didn't like this one bit. He thought tea was a waste of money and a destroyer of health, and he wrote an angry public letter against the practice. Thankfully, Jonas lost the battle, and the piping hot drink remained as popular as ever. Today, you can find his letter on display in Twinings, the oldest tea shop in London.

Despite what Mary Poppins may tell you, it wasn't much fun to be a chimney sweep in London—especially if you were a "climbing boy." Most chimneys were too small for a man to crawl into, so orphans were snatched off the street to do the job. Most of the boys were under the age of seven and received no pay. Some even got stuck in the chimneys! Jonas Hanway didn't like this one bit. He fought to protect the climbing boys, and even wrote an angry public letter against the practice. Thankfully, Jonas won the battle, and laws were passed to make it more difficult to engage the use of climbing boys. Unfortunately, it still took another hundred years for the practice to be completely outlawed in 1875.

A BRIEF HISTORY OF UMBRELLAS

2000s–1500s B.C.
Parasols are used
by nobility in Egypt.

1100s B.C.
Waterproof parasols (umbrellas)
are used by nobility in China.

481 B.C.
Buddha's funeral procession
is shaded by parasols.

500s–800s A.D.
The umbrella comes to Japan and
becomes a national art form.

400s B.C.
Parasols become a popular
item for women in Greece.

1500s
High-ranking Aztec soldiers
wear umbrella-shaped banners
as part of their uniform.

1660s
The umbrella comes
to France and becomes
a Parisian staple.

1719
Robinson Crusoe builds an umbrella
out of animal hide in Daniel Defoe's
novel, *Robinson Crusoe*.

1852
British industrialist
Samuel Fox invents the modern
steel-ribbed umbrella.

1830
James Smith & Sons opens in
London. Today, it is the oldest
umbrella store in Europe.

1750
Jonas Hanway shocks
Londoners by carrying
an umbrella.

1865
African American
inventor William
C. Carter invents
the umbrella stand.

1900s
German philosopher Friedrich Nietzsche
baffles scholars with a mysterious
sentence in his unpublished writings:
"I have forgotten my umbrella."

1926
Winnie-the-Pooh uses a
flipped-over umbrella as
a boat to rescue Piglet in
A. A. Milne's *Winnie-the-Pooh*.

1934
Mary Poppins uses an umbrella to
fly away from Number 12 Cherry
Tree Lane, London in P. L. Travers's
bestselling children's novel *Mary Poppins*.

1929
Polish artist Slawa Horowitz invents
the compact folding umbrella,
after asking, "Why on earth must
I carry this utterly clumsy thing?"

1952
Gene Kelly dances
with an umbrella
in the movie musical
Singin' in the Rain.

1997
Rubeus Hagrid uses an umbrella/wand
to give Dudley Dursley a pig's tail in
J. K. Rowling's worldwide bestseller,
Harry Potter and the Philosopher's Stone.

BIBLIOGRAPHY

Bellis, Mary. "Who Invented the Umbrella?" ThoughtCo., 2009. https://www.thoughtco.com/who-invented-the-umbrella-1992592.

Durack, Susan. "The Chimney-Sweeper's Friend." MU Library Treasures, July 7, 2015. https://mulibrarytreasures.wordpress.com/2015/07/07/the-chimney-sweepers-friend/.

Flint, Kate. "How Does English Weather Relate to National Identity?" The Guardian. Public Books, Guardian Books Network, October 2, 2016. https://www.theguardian.com/books/2016/oct/12/how-does-english-weather-relate-to-national-identity.

Look and Learn. "Hanway's Umbrella Gave Protection in the Wet British Weather." Historical Articles and Illustrations, April 13, 2013. https://www.lookandlearn.com/blog/23616/hanways-umbrella-gave-protection-in-the-wet-british-weather/.

Marshall, Ed, C.C.B, F.C. Birkbeck Terry, Everard Home Coleman, Duncan Pitcher, George Clulow, and Edward Walford. "Umbrellas Not Used in London in 1795." *Notes and Queries* (January–June 1896): 155–156.

Monasterio, Lucia Ortiz. "Meet the First Man Who Dared to Use an Umbrella." Aleph. FAENA, March 31, 2015. http://www.faena.com/aleph/articles/meet-the-first-man-who-dared-to-use-an-umbrella/.

Taylor, J. S. "Jonas Hanway: Pioneer Philanthropist." The Therapeutic Care Journal. The International Centre for Therapeutic Care, November 1, 2008. https://www.thetcj.org/child-care-history-policy/jonas-hanway-pioneer-philanthropist.

Walford, Edward. "Jonas Hanway, the Philanthropist." *The Gentleman's Magazine* 254 (January–June 1883): 296–303.

To David, who knows a good idea when he sees one.
— J. C.

To my parents, Bill and Jeanne Ryan, for instilling a
love of all the scandalous and silly stories history has to offer.
— E. R. E.

Text copyright © 2020 Josh Crute. Illustrations copyright © 2020 Eileen Ryan Ewen. First published in 2020 by Page Street Kids, an imprint of Page Street Publishing Co., 27 Congress Street, Suite 105, Salem, MA 01970, www.pagestreetpublishing.com. All rights reserved. No part of this book may be reproduced or used, in any form or by any means, electronic or mechanical, without prior permission in writing from the publisher. Distributed by Macmillan, sales in Canada by The Canadian Manda Group. ISBN-13: 978-1-62414-885-9. ISBN-10: 1-62414-885-9. CIP data for this book is available from the Library of Congress. This book was typeset in Cormorant Infant. The illustrations were done in ink and watercolor. Printed and bound in Shenzhen, Guangdong, China

20 21 22 23 24 CCO 5 4 3 2 1

trustees